MW00616329

Sober Man's Thoughts

William Bolyard

DEAD RECKONING

COLLECTIVE

20 17

TABLE OF CONTENTS

.................................15

Reflections 16

ul 17

nk 18

.................................19

.................................20

.................................22

l Stop This Train 23

oves 24

ound is an Odd Game 26

.................................27

ssues 28

.................................29

in the Mirror 30

.................................32

Bar 33

.................................38

of the Western World 40

son with a Sandstorm 41

.................................42

bee Night 45

nd 47

past Was Always There 48

es 50

Copyright © 2020 Dead Reckoning Collective, LLC

All rights reserved.
This book or any portion thereof
May not be used or reproduced in any fashion whatsoever
Without the permission of the publisher or the author
Except for the use of quotations

Publisher: Dead Reckoning Collective
Book Cover Art: Tyler James Carroll

First Edition: March 2021
Printed in the United States of America

ISBN-13: 978-1-7338099-6-2 (paperback)

This book is de
that served me
buddy of mine t
rambles, and mo
can never hold

This one's on

Split Wine

Cigarette

Troubled S

Endless Dr

Three A.M.

Drink More

Sober Pens

Someone Wil

One Night L

Bouncing Ar

Crowded Bar

Commitment

Fin ....

Reflections

Rooftops ...

Layers of a

Cheers .....

Similarities

Trying to Rea

The Bell ....

Bingo on a Ty

Dead Man's Ha

Call to the C

Midnight Grav

Broke Record 51

Bar 52

Fundamentals 54

If I Die 56

Hanging Up the Rifle 59

Hunting 60

Still With Me 62

Bottle Thoughts 63

Drive 64

This is the Life You Choose 66

Dried Bottles 67

Sunflower Girl 68

Bubba 69

Old Man 70

Short Story 71

Speech 72

Relationships 74

1/2 Priced Drinks in a Hurricane 75

Dogs 78

Fight 79

YAVIN 80

Fresh Encounters with a Woman 82

Tequila 84

1000 Stories with No One to Tell 85

Buzz Kill 87

Stoop 88

Poos 90

Birth 91

Soaked and Stoked 92

Refill 95

Coastal 96

Jim the Bartender 98

Back and Forth 100

Lessons 101

Red 102

Fists 104

Trash Puppies 105

Layover 106

Eye Contact 108

Just in Case 109

Dream Journal 110

Departures 113

Last Train to Dublin 114

A Sober Man's Thoughts 118

More Than a Beer 120

Gentle Hands 121

Prompt 122

Mania 126

Missed Calls 128

Nostalgic Hangover 130

Dirt Diamonds 132

Gun Case 134

Tilted Lampshade 136

I Hate This One 138

SPI 140

Melione 142

Chronological 143

60 Seconds 144

Old Times 145

Dream Catcher 146

Liquor Store Deli 147

Introduction

First things first: this is not going to be a happy book. It will be hard to read at most times, and if you have felt these same emotions or lived through any events of a similar nature, you will understand. This book has been something I've been working on for three years. Yet if I'm being frank, it has been about six years. This book is about how I dealt with the death of someone I loved more than life itself. I lived in a bottle; I traveled the world and did about every self-destructive act I could, all in an attempt to fill a hole in my heart that was going nowhere. These words are the things I could never say out loud. Things that lurk in the depths of our mind and dwell in the bottom of our hearts. I did not find god in these places and deeds. I did not get sober after a revelatory experience. This is not that book, nor will I ever write one on that subject, just like how I will never write a book like this again. There is no lesson here. So, don't look for it. The idea behind this book is very simple. Feel.

The idea behind it was born in the French Alps. I was recovering from a particularly brutal hangover, which tends to follow when you party with a bunch of Hungarians for a week and consume your bodyweight in moonshine. But during my recovery, I read a book. In that book, it told the story of a man always running from his past, making one wrong choice after another and never actually dealing with the issues. In the book, the author described emotions that I truly felt right down to my soul. I finished it in a single day, and after I did, I sat there for a full hour thinking about what I had just read. That book changed my life. I went to my roommate and told him right then that I was going to write a book. He didn't speak much English, so he didn't understand me. When I got home to my tiny apartment above a bar, I got to work. I started compiling all my drunken scribbles and journals. Then I read another book written by an equally great man, who told the story about how he sold all his things and moved to Central America. How he traveled the world, and through traveling, he was healed of life's past pain. That book changed my life.

I then meet these two authors at a strip club in Atlanta. They read poetry and shared drinks. I told them things all authors hear from fans:

"I'm thinking of writing a book."

"Oh yeah? About what"?

"Suicide, death, pain, and love."

They wished me the best of luck and told me to let them know when I finished.

I spent three years living a story. I wrote in bars, alleys, jail cells, and bedrooms. I lived and wrote everywhere from Havana to Marzari Sharif, a journey that spanned four continents and a war. I will be your bartender this evening. These poems I selected are enjoyed best over ice.

-William Bolyard

Spilt Wine

White shag rug

All the lights unplugged

The night engulfed in sin

I hope it never ends

Candles flicker on the glass

Both of us trying to erase our past

Purple rain playing on the turntable

Your touch and the drink make me stable

One night can change your life

But this one was just to keep us alive

<u>Cigarette Reflections</u>

The constant struggle for man

Is deciding if he wants to settle down

Or spend the night.

Troubled Soul

A troubled soul knows no end to his road.

He drinks and stomps he is no more.

He asks it to stop,

But keeps causing the pain

A relationship here, a selfish act there

Anything else to keep up the game.

Because at the end of the day

He knows the truth

He loves it,

He CRAVES it,

HE NEEDS IT!

A troubled soul knows no end to his road.

Endless Drink

I wish I had an endless drink

Deeper, deeper, deeper to help me sink.

Constantly would it push me to the brink

Endlessly, relentlessly, more whiskey…

Something to forever numb the pain

Something to finally make me sane.

Or is it just a suicidal dream?

Three A.M.

At three A.M. all rules are aside

You can drink,

You can laugh,

You may even cry.

'Cause at three A.M. the world is alive

For those who choose to reside in the rye.

Drink More

Drink more, it makes you better

Makes you clearer.

Whiskey cuts through

The smokey thoughts that cloud your mind

Drink more.

You know you're fine

You have handled worse and had more

Drink more.

The temptation on your shoulder

Is soothed by a sip

Nothing else can loosen this grip

The grip of reality, the grip of pain.

Drink more.

Cold steel is a ghastly taste of sobriety

It's not right

But it will bring you closer to her.

Drink one more.

Sober Pens

Not drunk enough to write

Damn, how is that right?

Easy rhymes to pass the time

Don't be a pussy, dive in deeper

It makes you think clearer

Bring up the darkness

Sulk in the liquor

Think on the words you never speak

Go ahead and wet your beak.

Someone Will Stop This Train

You ever been pulled in so many different
directions

That all you wanted to do is sleep with a
woman?

Thinking that somehow was the cure

Late night stumbling in the door

The bottle you brought home,

Spilling on the floor

You sit in the kitchen

Back against the cabinet

Your eye finds misery

Where the old letters are hidden

Guess my heart is that lonely

Your eyes read over old flames

Filling your heart with bleeding pain

You should go back out

Don't end the night like this

Find a girl

Chat her up

Beg her to somehow stop this train

One Night Loves

For the nights you spend out too late
Where you meet someone you should date
In a strange land you find each other
This must be fate
A girl who loves what you love

Knows things you know

And laughs at all your jokes
For the drinks and the smokes
The kisses and the music
You dance entwined in true happiness,

And love you're sure never passes
Sheets tangle all night, then you hold her
Through sun rise
Whispering how "this was the best night"
Kiss in the parking lot,
Leave your number in her hand,
Oh so clever
Little did you know
It was goodbye forever.

Bouncing Around is an Odd Game

Strange places and mostly decent food make
it all worth it, the local beer is also a
huge deciding factor.

By odd I mean the whole essence of it.

One airport turns to five,

And six drinks turn to a hundred.

A woman you spent passion filled nights with
will call you.

Saying she will be in your area by winter,

But you will be in Afghanistan.

Ironic one hell traded for the other.

Always on the go, never establish roots,
because men are not trees.

We grow weak the longer we stay in place.

To establish roots is to die;

Lose your personality;

Lose who you are.

To grow is to move;

To stay is to die

Crowded Bar

Loud music

Fast women

Stiff drinks

All I can think about is violence

My mind escapes to a different time

A time where things were simple and pure

Am I wrong?

Is this madness?

Or is this just the gin talking

I don't know

I don't care

All I know is that I need the rush.

Commitment Issues

Two days is all it takes

She is perfect but I must break

"I'm not ready,"

I lie

But at night

My loneliness burns a hole deep inside

The call to be free keeps me at bay

Like a ship with nowhere to stay

<u>Fin</u>

The pull to the rush

The pull of a trigger

Which of these will end me quicker?

Reflections in the Mirror

In my dreams I'm lost in time

Tumbling through my memories

Trying to find my dime

Open a door there

We're laughing in the car

My mind and my heart

Entrenched with deep scars

Stumble through

Replayed nightmares struggling to escape

A whisper of your voice jolts me awake

Cold sweats and empty beds

Are a sobering fate

Nights like these I struggle with reality

Worrying if this will be the death of me

Living with ghosts of a former life

Cold chills are beaten back by whisky

Drink, sleep, repeat.

Rooftops

Rolling dark coming across the moon

Like my mood

When the liquor seeps into my mind

Smoke rolls out my mouth

And the darkness seeps off my tongue

The only purity I know

Lives in bottles

And that's how I plan to keep it

Cold glass, hot thoughts

Layers of a Bar

You see that first bottle,

Pristine and presentable.

Give me three rows back

And I'll show you the real.

Battered, faded and passed around,

A friend when all is lost.

At the end of the bar

You will see it

The regular

Battered, faded and passed around

He knows all is lost

Yet he keeps coming back

Sharing wisdom when he can

See the layers of a bar

Are complex

Glass half empty

Might be a glass half full

A drunk old man

Might be your future

The beauty of the world resonates different
with a man who has lost his.

Any bar burning down is sad

Where will people like me go to worship?

Cheers

I don't like many bars,

But the bars I love are the real bars.

The bars with the jukebox,

The bars with the 1st class system

With the 3rd grade teacher talking about the terrible kids.

A drinking hole that has the back porch fading into the marsh.

A real bar is the cursing, drinking, dirty glass, fading light,

Blue collar man in a white-collar bottle.

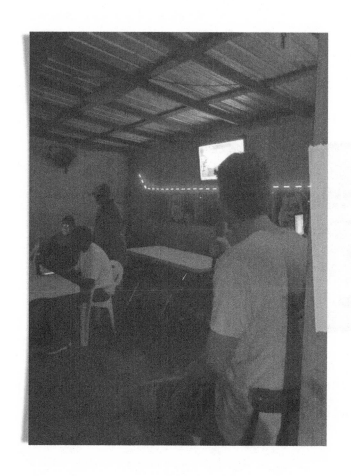

Similarities of the Western World

7 months gone

Orange lights and asphalt

A welcoming beacon.

Grass and cool summer nights

Crescent moon fading bright,

To a mid summer morning.

Industrial complexes all the same

Homecoming in a world abroad

Western from Eastern

Europe or Americas

Not so different to a man coming home.

Trying to Reason with a Sandstorm

Sometimes the wadies smelt like the harbor

Valley gusts felt like ocean breeze

At least the heat's the same.

But the birds are different here

Traded seagulls for Blackhawks

They carry a different weight

Both are home to my heart

Paradise is relative

The Bell

Brass and old

Loud and bold

I wish I knew the stories you told

Dents and digs

You no longer ring

Oh, how I'd love to know what you've seen

Sadly

Tropical lands are not kind on old metal

Cigar smoke sure can soften the leather

Caller of important gatherings

Maybe those of revolutionaries

A pillar of this pilgrims' journey

In the rain on papa's estate

Pictures are all I would take

People with sad backgrounds

Make the best creationists

Because we are constantly

Trying to create

A different existence.

Bingo on a Tybee Night

Out of beer, so I stumbled to a bar across
the street. Locals fill the watering hole,
I'm the center of attention when I stroll
in. Like a different species, they know I'm
not one of them, but it's 5-dollar bingo
night so they need the extra wager. $1
drafts and $5 bets, a place I can get along
with. What more do you need? As the only
attractive girl in the bar makes
conversation and turns the wheel. I sip on
cheap beer. Normal Sunday night.

I'm a dead and lonely man. Trapped in the casket of a man with a purpose.

Dead Man's Hand

I'm the man you will sleep with,

But never marry

The thought of forever all too scary

I just need this tonight

A short fix to a lasting loneliness

Heroin to a longing heart.

Your eyes will be the key

Into my drunken soul

My true self,

A bad hand dealt

A man empty and dull.

So please don't love me

Keep me warm

But let me stay cold.

Call to the Coast Was Always There

When I was a boy, it was the salt air

As a man, it was the breeze and the waves.

Maturity brings respect for the sea

Wonderment for its mysteries

Enchantment of its travels.

The very same I felt as a boy.

I am an old soul with the sea

Mesmerized by her beauty,

I realize she is the woman for me

I was not born with her

But I will die with her.

Engulfed by the surf,

Swept out with the tide.

Picture perfect black and white,

With a board by my side.

Midnight Graves

Side by side

One for me

One for you

Side by side

Staring at the moon

I talk

You listen

Tombstones never reply

Broke Record

Closure is for the dying

Leave on a broke record

It gives you a reason to live

A damaged door to fix

Some chance to save your soul

Bar

Warm beer

Stale cigarettes

I didn't need company

But here you are

Go get two drinks

Gone

A cure dripped away

Two drinks for me

Light a smoke

Fade to black

Scene

Fundamentals

Man is easier to shoot than dogs

Animals are long, man is tall

Never will you mess up with the rise or fall

If I Die

Here's to the boys,

Thanks for the long nights and being beside
me in the roughest fights

Hope to not see you too soon.

Don't linger on the past and make life great
my cheery buffoons

And when you drink one for me down at
Shabooms

Make sure to leave with the most beautiful
date.

Here's to the girls,

Oh, how I loved to make you twirl.

Smokey taverns and endless nights.

Sadly, I could never love you right.

My heart was elsewhere

In a war

Or my only girl.

Thanks for the time well wasted

Now find a man, that won't regret it.

Here's to my mother,

Never will I be able to repay you for the
things you've done.

You raised me alone as your first son.

Against all odds you made a man.

Hope I made you proud in the end.

Don't cry,

I died doing what I loved,

with true warriors from above

Please find my brother

Tell him I'm sorry

He deserved so much better.

Here's to my love,

Soon we will be together again,

The only good thing from my end.

We can make a new life in whatever is on the
other side.

Hold me tight for I know it's finally the
end of my fight.

Here's to the man,

That took my life.

Hope you fought proud and true,

honestly thought I'd never lose.

I wish you only good fortune and fame

Cause I know I would have done the same.

To all the others,

I failed to mention,

Go fuck yourself.

Glad you listened.

Hanging Up the Rifle

The war is over

Time for some sweet closure

Served proud and true

In a faraway land next to you

The honor was mine

Completing every task superior to fine

A true master of your craft

A warrior that helped bring us back

Whatever you find in your next profession

Nothing will follow but many blessings

Thank you, brother,

From me and all the others

Reside to your paradise tide

The war is over

I know you won't need closure

Hunting

I think I'm done

But it gnaws at me

Hemingway once said,

"The hunting of man" is the greatest game

For me it's an addiction

And I can't stop the crave

The violence is my drug

The rush my sickness

Success in combat

Is unparalleled to anything

One could achieve

In a single lifetime

It's earning your right to live

And taking another's away

Still With Me

It was usually just the past

Dreams of different realities with her as my guide

My own ghost of Christmas present

She warns

I promise

I wake

Bottle Thoughts

I believe in one true love

But number two keeps me up

She has golden hair

That matches her ring

And a heart that broke at seventeen

Drive

I will break my back for a piece of metal

Stay up long days for success

Work long hours to be better

But

I will not put effort into love

Would rather be alone than try

Suffer alone than reach

That is my edge

That is the curse

This is the Life You Choose

That's what you thought I suppose

The words a loud echo

Spoken by a man

Who began my journey long ago

Sleepless nights

Broken body

Mangled souls

Rocky roads

I never truly would know

Until two days of fighting

With nowhere to go

Two brothers gone

Many more in between here and beyond

Lying in bed a moment of clarity

Those words echo in my head

"This is the life you choose"

7 years later I still don't know

When will I find an exit on this road?

Dried Bottles

The ink's dried at the bottom

Just like my empty bottles

Happiness kept it all away

Like a warm breeze in the Atlantic bay

... Storms come just like that

And I'm not beating down the hatch

Uncork the wine and clean the glass

Because I believe it's time to bleed

Sunflower Girl

Barefoot to a funk jam

Like a scene out of a classic film

Shook and swayed to a beat no one else
danced

She stole the venue

From a R&B crew

A sunflower girl will steal your soul

Leave you wishing for a never-ending evening

And leave your heart with a nonstop feeling

Bubba

Regular

A title earned Like a rank

New place to drink

Becomes a home of smiles to savor

New friends, old drinks,

And a harbor to wash it down

Bartender plays chess in between orders

Sailors swap stories

Customers shoot whiskey

Sometimes bars become homes

And sometimes it's better to rock the boat

Old Man

Light a smoke

Tell a joke

Order a beer

Wipe a tear

"Where you been?"

"Who's your kin?"

Old man shares a smoke

Tells a joke

"Have a Miller"

"Can tell you're a killer"

Take a gulp

Cold and hot

Been here a lot

"Don't live in it forever

It fades like burnt paper "

Old leather looks a lot like scared skin

Tells a story most can't comprehend

Short Story

Send reinforcements soon

Young men preferred

Speech

Story of a man's life is told three times.

Once at his wedding by his best man,

A couple times at his funeral,

by people that loved him,

And forever after his death,

by the life that he lived.

Relationships

Relationships are about timing.

Where you are in your life,

Who you are in life

And what you want to be in life.

A woman could be perfect,

But she might not be the right time,

I believe that there is no right or wrong woman

It's just what similar traits are found

At the time your spirit is ready to settle.

For some it comes quicker than others.

Outside influences, such as

Death, heartbreak, gain, love and true happiness

Affect all these factors of the perfect mate.

The you from five years ago is an inner shell of who you are now,

Because of your outer experience.

Layers upon layers of your heart are built over time.

And time and loneliness are the only things that will truly settle that

Or... true euphoric love.

But that is nothing but sunshine and rainbows.

1/2 Priced Drinks in a Hurricane

Pots, pans and turntables

Jimmy Buffett and drinking enables

12 drinks deep

To the bar I want to seep

Hurricane party is on the creeps

Half-dressed blonde dame

Hurricane won't stop this train

Eating street food is how you maintain your nomad card.

Dogs

A dog molds a boy's soul into adulthood,
imprints in him a guide through his wild
heart. Like a girl will have a doll and
learn to nurture through inanimate
affection, a boy will have his pup. Together
they will mature into young adulthood.
Learning together how to navigate the world.
As the boy ages the dog will too. Finally,
when the boy climbs into early adulthood,
the dog will teach the man one final lesson.
Loss. Loss and death of his closest, oldest
friend. Then, and only then will he be ready
for the world...

Fight

Don't trust a man who's not willing to get
punched in the face

<u>YAVIN</u>

Howlers through the trees

Make sure to leave them be

Trees and vines

Much different than pines

The jungle is unforgiving

Mayan temples

Out they come peaking

Macaws next to me

Sunset on the top of trees

Damn... what a sight

The rebels sure knew how to fight

Fresh Encounters with a Woman

Dance and dine

Central American music plays

Shook a hand

Danced a jig

Rum and pheromones fuel this

Bump

BUMP

Strange man cuts in

Quick Talk

Solves it up

Dance

DANCE

Senorita won't leave this to chance

Tequila

Agave

What a strange plant

I thought with another shot

1000 Stories with No One to Tell

Lived a life worth sharing

Between the liquor and the fighting

I used to tell you everything

But now I drink in a cemetery

I share

You listen

Sure, you heard them once or twice

But, I know you like to hear about my life

I'm a drunk with a keen sense for sobriety

Buzz Kill

Coffee

Black

Cup of ice

2 sugars

Was my go-to

Would pull me out of a semi haze

Where I would debate drinking time

Either to work

Or to the bar

Finances would decide the rest

Stoop

Waiting for a maybe death

Cars fly by

Rum dries up

The night was a slump

Lost a key

Nothing left to see

I finish my drink like the best

Softly wish for death

I want it to end

But I know I haven't had enough sin

The worst is abandonment

From a woman with harsh resentment

Another man took your place

Can't always be an ace

Life is about the balance of gambling,

What you win,

And what you're willing to lose

Poos

I think what made the bar so unique was the staff. They created the atmosphere that was the bar. Saturday nights the off crew would play funk music, and I mean really play. The rest of the staff would make it their business to have a conversation with everyone: tourist, local, bachelorette party- it didn't matter. Everyone got a welcome fretting from poos. Dollar bills so old on the walls they were completely faded gray; the outdoor patio was covered partially from an old sail and on packed nights it was just a giant party on the deck. Nothing like it really. Words can't describe the camaraderie of this tribe of island drinkers; tighter than most ship crews I've met.

Birth

I was born in a bar

I was conceived in a bottle

And my womb was open credit

I was birthed in a glass

Out into the cold, hard world

Surrounded by my friends

My true blood

There I was raised

Alone some nights

Social most

But I was truly coming of age

Sometimes in the bathroom with a woman

Another in a brawl on the steps

Each sharing its own lesson

A back alley was the road home

To sobriety or debauchery

Soaked and Stoked

Sun fading

Beer following

Waves frothing

Can't remember a better day

Blessed to have the ocean allow me to ride

My final love will be her

Pour a drink into the tide

Until next time

I've shared more nights with cheap drink and dry tobacco, than I have with any women.

Refill

I've lived in a gutter.

I've dined in castles.

But my greatest moment

Was sharing my heart with you.

Coastal

On the coast everything is a little broken

The island is always in a state of disrepair

Few people are from it

If they are,

Their parents definitely weren't

Cold coastal coasts

Are full of people fleeing from the past

Must be the breeze

Or the brown tall grass

It's home though

To those with none

Guess that's why I fit in

Jim the Bartender

I read this magazine from my dad's bathroom when I was younger. Stashed between a couple of Playboys that I visited frequently. In the magazine, was a recurring segment called Jim the Bartender, the articles were just normal guy issues. Issues ranged from, "how to ask this girl out?" to "should I go to the doctor about this?" and even "what do I do if my kid isn't mine?" When I was a boy, I would read these and think "damn, can't wait to have my own bartender." Strange thoughts for a boy, but if you see how I live now, it would make sense. Well in all of my years of drinking I never found my Jim. I guess the art has been lost in the age of phones, swipes, and Tripadvisor. That was until I meet Howie. Howie was a bartender at a bar on the island where the sailors drank. The bar was built right on the dock, where you could watch otters play right on the outdoor patio. It was a hard to find place and most people didn't even know it was there but the people there were genuine and they took me in as the weathered drinker I am. I met Howie two days back from Afghanistan, sat down at the bar and ordered a gin and lime juice. Now I'm very particular about it because people always mess it up by adding tonic water and artificial lime juice to it, when it's literally just gin and fresh lime juice. Think I found the recipe in an old cocktail book somewhere. Well, Howie knew it by name.

98

"Ah! You mean a gin Gimlet!" I knew right then I had found my Jim.

Back and Forth

I want to fight

I want to die

I want to live forever

Never satisfied

Always chasing something

Mystified by the call of death

Addicted to violence

Satan's heroin

I know it doesn't make sense

What does?

<u>Lessons</u>

I read this on a drunk tank wall

"Don't fight cops

Unless they are off duty

Then they are human"

Red

You mesmerize me

As if kissed by an Atlantic sunrise

Your hair radiates my passion

No lies are told in our conversation

Back to your place for a music session

Turning my head for a final glimpse

While I creep out from an all night event

You will thank me later, I promise you this

Fists

A man should not fear a fight

The trading of fists is a sacred art

Born almost at the dawn of time

The meta of one true fate

Original source of survival

Bone and flesh

Served as thought and judgement

Modern times

Humans fear conflict

Turned from primitive times

Blood dropped is a mortal sin

Talk and persuade are righteous

In a time of turn the other cheek

We should hold on to our early times

Or risk losing it all together

Trash Puppies

Buried in yogurt and wires

Yelping and mangy

We feed them cookies and tangy energy

You pulled them out

Washed the fur

Moved them to something more sure

Most wouldn't have cared

But you did

Swapped tales of adventure and fright

Talked about the mission tomorrow night

See you later brother

But I never did

I promise you,

I won't forget

Layover

You never know what your last message will
be.

So, spell it out and check it twice on the
flight,

Because it might be read at a funeral.

Eye Contact

I could try a million times

Look into a million eyes

But never can I

Replace your soul I've stared inside

Just in Case

Drive by the old house

Drink a beer by the lake

Just in case

Damn what a moon

Know I'm leaving soon

Hell, what do I have to lose?

Just in case

Walk by her house

My "should have been"

Catch a glimpse

Just in case.

Dream Journal

This one was different. I had been gone and she had awoken from a coma. All my life events were the same but she had awoken while I was overseas. She had met another man, but when I came home, she left him immediately for me. Then it was just like it used to be, us on the couch, laughing kissing, holding each other and I was able to be open with someone for the first time in a very long time. She held me like she used to- really held me. I could feel her arms wrap around me, and I could feel her warmth. She didn't want to make love. I agreed, but I wanted to so bad. I missed her so much in every way. I left back for the Army.

When I came back, some time had passed and she was sitting there by the lake. One empty wooden chair beside her and another man. I sat in the empty chair held her hand. The man said nothing and had no face. She told me she couldn't choose between him and I. She told me I lived in a place she couldn't visit and that I had changed so much. We both had changed. I knew it. I told her I would go with her, begged her, pleaded like I have never plead before. I cried with my face buried in her lap. She kissed my forehead and told me "I can't come, but I will always love you and always be there." She walked away with that man in the fog.

I awoke in a hotel room. Empty, dark, and cold. I laid there in thought with dried tears on my face. I wonder if I will ever feel that happy again, or if it's possible to feel that amount of love from someone else. I doubt it, but I have hope because that's all you can do. I think about the last time I went and visited her. I don't visit like I used too. I left a beer can on her headstone. She never really drank beer, but it's a thing I've been doing for 6 years, so it's not one of those things I am trying to change. I wonder if she knows.

Ain't nothing wrong with writing for beer

Departures

The sun is high

The wings match

Up here no bird sings

Rope is tight

I feel no fright

Sip the drink

Take the plunge

Last Train to Dublin

It was a rainy hungover morning in Ireland's capital. My friends and I stumbled out of the hostel looking for food. Completely unaware of the town we had spent the last two days binge drinking in, we got lost. After many wrong turns down old wet streets we stumbled upon the Guinness factory. "Liquid breakfast it is!", my buddy yelled as he skipped towards the entrance. It didn't sound like a terrible idea, so I followed. Along the way through the brewery, I asked an old Irish man, "How far is it to Athlone from here?", he replied, "Oh, only about an hour and a half train ride." I was ecstatic. See in the small Irish town Athlone, in the city square next to the old castle, sits the world's oldest bar, Sean's Bar. It was also my own personal pilgrimage for my whole European adventure. I told the crew, and they were immediately on board. I mean, who wouldn't want to see that. We checked the train schedule, and sure enough, the last train was leaving in about two hours, and the last train to Dublin from Athlone left at Nine at night. Plenty of time to finish the tour, catch the train and get good an drunk at Sean's before the last train left the station.

At the top of the gravity bar, I had my first Guinness. See I never had a taste for the dark drink but I figured the home of the porter would be the only fitting place. As I looked over the Dublin dreary skyline, a feeling of true happiness over came me. It felt odd in my bones because for so long I had been empty without any emotion, let alone happiness. Maybe this was the beginning of a change. As I finished my drink my friends introduced me to another group of travelers. We had a couple more pints, swapped tales of adventure and wrong doing as time slipped away. "Hey mate, how far is the train station from here?", I asked through a gulp of Guinness. "Don't worry, man, it's only a mile and a half we have plenty of..." he was cut off from his own desperate look at his watch. I knew immediately what that meant; in one sweeping motion I slammed my drink and headed for the door. Mid stride keeping the pace my two companions handed me their glasses. Not wanting to see the waste of two perfectly poured brews I finished both of them without losing stride. Not ideal for a thick drink.

With a belly full of beer, our feet hit the cobblestone at top speed. I was wearing cowboy boots with Levi jeans, so how I was moving so quickly is still a mystery. We crossed through the station in nine minutes, bought our tickets in two, short pit stop to puke on the tracks, and found our seats with one minute to spare. As the train took off, I saw a couple of sheep enjoying a bright green lunch of Irish countryside. By the time we arrived, it was three o'clock in the afternoon. Which left us with about six hours to drink and catch our ride home. We all agreed that we would keep better track of time this go around, so there was no need to rush. The station was barren; the only people we found were the janitor and the ticket lady. We asked both for the directions to Sean's Bar; they both pointed towards the front entrance of the station. I had remembered seeing pictures of it next to a castle so I told my group it was probably best to head towards the city square. It being the oldest bar in the world I was sure there would be a sign or two showing us the way. Short brisk walk down the dingy sidewalk and we see the castle. Well, what was left of it at least but no sign or placard for the bar. We circle the block, still nothing. "I'm going to swing into that place with the giant toucan mural to see if they know where it's at," I yelled to my two companions who were off peeping corners together, but that is another story. As I get closer, I see some small white lettering underneath some hanging ferns. "GUYS, QUICK, I FOUND IT."

Under the giant toucan with little to no markings was the world's oldest bar. As we stroll in two mangy mutts scurry across the floor. Gaelic music plays in the back where two old Irish men go on about how they hate Muslims. Guess it's the same as any small-town bar. We grabbed a drink in a small corner booth and proceeded to chat and marvel at this place. I sipped on the house mead, which was original recipe from 900 A.D, it wasn't that great honestly but they left you a good buzz. With two friends that were becoming strangers and a couple strangers that were becoming friends I started to see the point behind it all. The source of my new found happiness was experience not companionship. My pilgrimage was complete, and I had a real sense of awakening.

We would end up almost missing our train again after a few too many house meads. Luckily my old boots hold the land speed record for Irish streets. When we settled in to our night train back to the city. I pulled out a flask I had saved for moments just like this. We passed it around in our own form of communion. We finished it quickly, and my two flat mates passed out wrapped up in each other. I looked out the black window on the last train to Dublin, reflecting on how euphoric traveling is for the soul. How it creates bonds with complete strangers and shows you the true nature of others. It opens your eyes to different cultures all while making you appreciate yours. "God damn.", I whispered to myself as I slide a beer a beer from my pocket I had swiped from the bar. I lifted my drink to the dark Irish countryside and drifted further into thought.

A Sober Man's Thoughts

I was too busy living life

To actually ever write it

Then one day I drank

And I felt

And I wept

I gathered the courage to heal

Finally finding a cure in the bottle

Knowing I couldn't continue

Corked up like rare whiskey

So, I grabbed a pen

And started to document

A sober man's thoughts

I wish I had an endless drink

deeper, deeper, deeper it would help me shit
Constantly would it push me to the brink
endlessly, relentlessly, make whiskey
Sonthing to forturd numb the pain
Sonthing to finally make my soul
Or is that just a suicidal dream

Maybe your mine

You were born in June
that I know is true
to a mom and a dad who would rais you right
but Wait theirs more
because 9 months before, me and mum shaked a night
but alas mum clamed him not me
I should tell glee and cheer
but when I saw your pictere, of you my maybe son
all my heart felt was sorrow...and despair
because maybe your mine
and maybe like your father, im like mine.

More Than a Beer

I told you I wouldn't write this

But you knew that wasn't true

How do you thank a man you owe everything to?

I slept on your couch when my life was shit

We chugged a pint of whiskey to make it all make sense

We fought together and you never winced

On that rooftop, in a cold bloody night

You saved my life,

With more bravery than I could ever write

You bought your shots from a bolt action rifle

I'm just trying to fill the bottle

Brother, I just want you to know

That I can never repay the debt I owe

And no matter how many years

I owe you more than a beer

Gentle Hands

Smooth

Calm

Breath…

Soft skin meets rough tin

Focus

Acquire

Breath…

Hard thoughts create smooth shots

Squeeze

Follow through

Breath…

Relax

Sit

Spit

Breath…

Look out at crimson stained sand

Created by gentle hands

Prompt

She was never boring

She was brave

I had it all

Now I speak to a grave

No solution was ever found in the bottle of
self-pity

Mania

Nothing is better than madness
No purer thing than crazy
I love it when the madness comes out
True is the mind
Fast is the thoughts
When it emerges from its hidden corners
Beauty is found
Buried underneath the bloody thoughts
Covered with painful memories
And tears
But
I love it when the madness comes out
The liquor taste better
My pen flows cleaner
Hidden demons pull up a seat
And grab a drink
They whisper thoughts that were always there
Sometimes they write a line down
I LOVE IT WHEN THE MADNESS COMES OUT
I murder my sober self on site
Him and his normal shell
The street display he is lies breathless on
the floor
BECAUSE WHEN THE MADNESS COMES OUT
I CAN FINALLY BREATHE
I CAN BE ALIVE!!!!
But then it fades
Like an old love letter
Words become blurred and passion fades
Too strong is the drink of madness
Not your everyday poison
When the madness fades
A man can finally sleep
And wait
For the return

Missed Calls

Stopped calling
I knew it was pointless
Too many times
Too many problems
I understand
You can't bear my world on your shoulders,

Or your heart...

New habits have been found
Now I write it all down
Realize complaining is for clowns
On your kitchen floor I knew
That I had nothing else to lose
So, I found the door
Peered into my core
Turned drink to ink
Death to life
All because I saw
Too many missed calls

Nostalgic Hangover

Took a sip from a glass

Just to make my mind crash

Upon emotions from the past

Dirt Diamonds

White gold stitched in red

Trash talk to keep your street cred

Bases loaded

So are the players

Wind up

Then the pitch

Sloppy, fast ball down the middle

Swing and a hit by just a little

Hit to the field with tons of errors

Thinking of times when we were better

In the park and around the bags

Beer break to fill the lags

Play till sundown because we had no lights

Then to the parking lot to drink all night

We were far from our prime but that's okay

We would play

In those dirt diamonds all damn day

Gun Case

I've been civilized for far too long

Cooped up and kept like the family rifle

Yet I'm unclean and loaded

Usually I'm not

At least not anymore

But on nights like this I can't help it

The emptiness calls out to me

I need to be fired

Shot into the night

I don't care at what

I just need a target

Tilted Lampshade

Sunlight breaking through the window

I awake from a dream of pure sorrow

Dried blood sticks to my sheets

From a run I thought I could beat

Grab last night's bottle

To wash out this morning's taste

Just another hostel

On the road to self-destruction

My desire and destination

Are oh so different

I Hate This One

Come in and out of my life

Like mist off the river

Or a midnight kiss

Slide into my mind

Like bad times

Or an unjust crime

Slip through arms

Like a venomous snake

Or mislead fate

Fast and heavy

Right but wrong

I want you

But we are not the right tune

We just play a different song

SPI

Didn't catch a single wave

Crushed a can threw it away

Pondered what was left of my life

Left or right

Fight or flight

Straight and narrow

I don't know

Broken heart and empty glasses

Is all that ever passes

Not a terrible way to keep time

I thought of you

As the sun crested the waves

Wondered who I'd be

If you were still with me

I don't know

My mind brought me back to a car ride

One filled with laughter and the future

Unlike the normal

With silence and the present

I swear

The salt air brought a whiff of your perfume

But I don't know

That's usually a sign to leave

Grabbed my board and sorrow

Made sure not to forget my towel

Where do I go

To the bar or home alone

Damn I really don't know

Melinoe

I thought of you yesterday

So, I drank

And spent all night forgetting

Chronological

When I was born my father left

At 8 I lost my first fight

I turned 13 in a jail cell

16 was when I would meet my old man

The army took me in at 18

At 20 years old I buried the love of my life

She too fought a silent fight

23 I was notifying families

Of their own tragedy

I killed my first man

Right before I turned 25

And I would drop out of college before 26

Ups but mostly downs

An old young man

I don't want your pity,

Neither your sympathy

Just want you to understand

The timeline of a lost man

60 Seconds

Let's drink until the ice runs out

Until you make me scream and shout

When the source is gone

And the record plays on

Let's excite and entice

Maybe we will find the meaning of life

Old Times

Old bar tops

Tell stories

But few listen

They see the scuffs

And drink stains

But not the pain

Not the end of the road

Down on the luck

Drink 'til my last buck

They only see

What they wish to see

Listen closely

You can hear the future

It says you will get better

Dream Catcher

Blonde hair basking in the moonlight

Dream catcher on your leg

Pulling me in

Catching my imagination

With broken minded sin

If I dive into your dream catcher

Will it capture me

Or pass me through like river water

Hippie girl, show me the truth

Let us build on our wild youth

Liquor Store Deli

"Wrap it up, I'll eat it here"

I sit down and sip my beer

Two days back off a fresh arrest

From a wild night I won't protest

Brush the sand from my hair

I think back

Back to a tequila moonlit night

Beautiful woman on my right

Played in the ocean

Skin on skin

Rolled on the sand making fresh new sin

Blonde hair flowing with the music

She sure knew how to use it

Cops would pick us up,

Too much drink underway

I would get taken away

She picked me up just past one

Stayed up all night till the rising sun

I know she will never be my wife

But her eyes keep me up at night

Finish my sandwich

Buy a bottle

Got to go home and finish a novel

This concludes three years of bar thoughts and drunken scribbles. Never hesitate to share your story with a stranger.

Last call...

DEAD RECKONING

20 17

COLLECTIVE

Dead Reckoning Collective is a veteran owned and operated publishing company. Our mission encourages literacy as a component of a positive lifestyle. Although DRC only publishes the written work of military veterans, the intention of closing the divide between civilians and veterans is held in the highest regard. By sharing these stories it is our hope that we can help to clarify how veterans should be viewed by the public and how veterans should view themselves.

Visit us at

deadreckoningco.com

Facebook: @deadreckoningco
Instagram: @deadreckoningcollective
Twitter: @dr_collective

William Bolyard is a man who enjoys traveling to strange lands, losing most his money at cards, drinking the other half away and occasionally getting in a fight over one of those subjects. He also writes.

He also has served as an infantryman for 8 years, and has deployed, and liked the food a lot.

Made in the USA
Monee, IL
19 April 2021

66196652R00090